D0473880

# LOONS

*Diving Birds* of the North

## DONNA LOVE

*Illustrated by* **Joyce Mihran Turley**
"Loonphabet" letters by Donna Love

Mountain Press Publishing Company
Missoula, Montana
2003

MONTROSE REGIONAL LIBRARY
320 SO. 2ND ST.
MONTROSE, CO 81401

Text © 2003 by Donna Love
Illustrations © 2003 by Joyce Mihran Turley, Dixon Cove Design
*All rights reserved*

Second Printing, August 2006

Library of Congress Cataloging-in-Publication Data

Love, Donna, 1956–
  Loons : diving birds of the North / Donna Love ; illustrated by Joyce Mihran
Turley, "Loonphabet" letters by Donna Love.—1st ed.
       p.   cm.
Includes bibliographical references.
  ISBN 0-87842-482-2 (pbk.  :  alk. paper)
  1. Loons—Juvenile literature. [1. Loons.]  I. Turley, Joyce Mihran, ill.  II. Title.
QL696.G33L68  2003
598.4'42—dc22
                                                                          2003012464

PRINTED IN HONG KONG BY MANTEC PRODUCTION COMPANY

Mountain Press Publishing Company
P.O. Box 2399, Missoula, Montana 59806
406-728-1900

*For my husband, Tim, and for my children, Nathan, Laura, and Aaron John, and for Alisa, who would have loved loons* —Donna

*For Rick, who gave me the time to paint by being such a good husband to me and a good father to our three children, Jeff, Kimberly, and Nate* —Joyce

## ACKNOWLEDGMENTS

I would like to thank Dr. Judith McIntyre, world-renowned loon researcher, for sharing her extensive knowledge of loons with us; wildlife biologist and educator Lynn Kelly, "Montana's Loon Lady," for her knowledge of loon behavior; wildlife biologists Susan Ball and Dennis Olson for their knowledge of loon physiology; illustrator Joyce Turley for her delightful images; and the staff of Mountain Press, specifically Kathleen Ort for her faithfulness, Lee Esbenshade for her edits, and Lynn Purl for pulling it all together. I would also like to thank the teachers and staff of Seeley Lake Elementary in Seeley Lake, Montana, for their support. Finally, my special thanks to the students of Seeley Lake Elementary for being my most helpful, enthusiastic teachers. —Donna

I am very grateful to Donna Love for her technical expertise, as she reviewed my sketches and paintings for accuracy. Editor Lynn Purl also served as art director, offering direction, support, and enthusiasm as the project progressed. I also must thank my high school art teacher, Frank Vurraro, for helping me to find my true colors! —Joyce

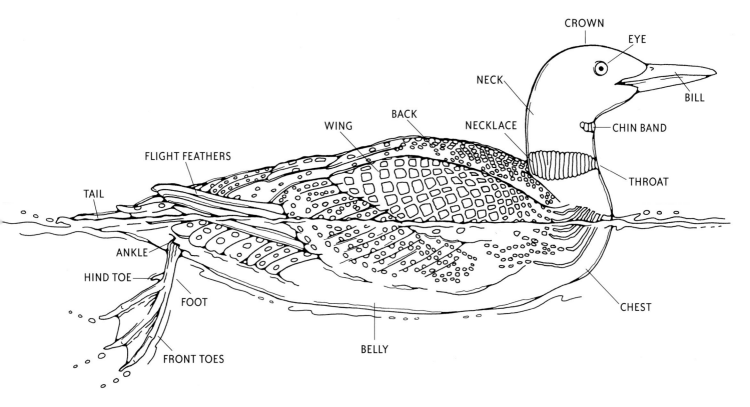

CROWN

EYE

NECK

BILL

BACK

WING

NECKLACE

CHIN BAND

FLIGHT FEATHERS

THROAT

TAIL

ANKLE

HIND TOE

FOOT

CHEST

FRONT TOES

BELLY

**W**hat bird dives like a submarine, flies like a jet, and wears a checkerboard on its back? A loon!

A loon is a fish-eating, diving bird that lives in the Northern Hemisphere, the part of the earth north of the equator. In summer a loon raises its chicks on northern fresh-water lakes. For the winter, it migrates to the ocean. How does a loon live in its cold-water world? To find out, let's explore this marvelous diving bird of the north.

# iving Hunter

A loon is a **predator**, an animal that hunts and eats other animals. Its **prey** — what it eats — is mainly fish, but it will also eat other **aquatic**, or water, creatures. In summer, in addition to fish, a loon may eat salamanders, crayfish, frogs, leeches, insects, and snails. In winter on the ocean, it adds crabs and shellfish to its diet of fish.

Loons belong to the order of birds called **Gaviiformes** (gah-vee-ih-FOR-meez). The **genus**, or group name, *Gavia* (GAH-vee-ah), is Latin for "seabird." There are five **species**, or kinds, of loons: the yellow-billed loon, common loon, Pacific loon, Arctic loon, and red-throated loon.

# Calls of the Wild

A loon is famous for its loud, haunting calls, which carry for miles over the water's surface. A common loon has four different calls. The **tremolo** is a laughlike call to show that the loon is afraid. The **wail** sounds like the howl of a wolf and is used to warn of danger or call a mate or young. The **hoot** sounds like an owl's hoot and lets the loon tell other loons where it is. Each male loon also has a unique **yodel**, a call that sounds like a seagull's cry, to defend its territory. The yellow-billed loon has calls similar to a common loon's. Pacific and Arctic loons make a variety of calls including a purrlike tremolo and a yodel by the males. Red-throated loons follow high-pitched wails with a tremolo that sounds like a duck's quacks.

A loon's ears are small openings on the sides of its head, covered by feathers. Scientists know by the inner shape of the ear that a loon can hear well. A loon may be able to recognize another loon's unique voice.

 # oon Lore

Loons appeared on earth about 65 million years ago, around the time the dinosaurs died out. Loons are among the oldest living birds in North America, so some bird books begin with loons. But people have enjoyed loons since long before books were written. Inuit (Eskimos) carved loons out of walrus ivory and made wooden loon masks for ceremonies. Some Inuit tribes consider loons sacred and do not hunt them.

Many people have believed that loons have magical powers. A story from Siberia tells of a loon that dove to the bottom of the sea and brought back mud on its foot to make the first land. In Europe some believed loons guided the souls of the dead to the afterworld. In America the Ojibwa (oh-JIB-way) Indians considered it a good sign to hear a loon call before a battle. The Cree believed the loon's call was the cry of slain warriors.

Today the loon is the state bird of Minnesota. In Ontario, Canada, schoolchildren chose the loon to be their provincial bird. Canada has a one-dollar coin with a picture of a loon on it. The coin is called a "loony."

# re Loons Loony?

Loons might do things that seem loony or silly to us, but the name *loon* does not mean silly. No one is certain where the word *loon* came from. It might be from the Scandinavian word *lomr,* which means "to mourn or lament," referring to the loon's sad-sounding calls. Or it might come from the Old English word *lumme,* meaning clumsy, which might refer to how awkwardly a loon moves on land. An English word, *loom,* means "track of a fish." Maybe the loon's name tells of its ability to chase and catch fish.

The Ojibwa called the loon *mahng,* which means brave. In Mexico, where some loons spend their winters, the loon is known as *el somorgujo* (soh-mohr-GOO-hoh), from the Spanish *somorgujar,* meaning "to dive." The French term for loon is *le plongeon,* which means "the diver." In Britain the loon is called a diver, and the common loon is known as the great northern diver.

# nderwater Eyes

An adult loon has red eyes. The color of its eyes tells other loons that it is of breeding age and may help it attract a mate. Even though the red eyes are striking above the surface, water filters light—and colors—out. The deeper a loon dives, the less red its eyes look. Under about fifteen feet of water a loon's eyes look gray.

During a dive a loon closes a thin layer of clear tissue called the **nictitating** (NIK-tih-tay-ting) **membrane** over each eye. The membranes work like swimming goggles to protect the loon's eyes from dirt and the sting of saltwater. Above water the membranes blink to clean the eyes. They also close during flight to keep the loon's eyes moist. When a loon sleeps it closes its outer eyelids upward over its eyes.

# ise Wardrobe

How many outfits do you have? A loon has two, and the male and female dress exactly alike. In summer, an adult loon wears the bold pattern of its **breeding plumage**, or mating feathers. The bold colors may help it attract a mate. In autumn a loon will **molt**, or lose its feathers, and grow the duller colored feathers of its **winter plumage**.

The loon's coloring may also **camouflage,** or hide, the bird from predators. From above, the loon's black-and-white spots look like sunlight shimmering on the water's surface to its summer predators, bald eagles. The loon's winter plumage matches the colors of the ocean, which helps camouflage it where sharks and orca whales lurk. A loon's colors may also help it sneak up on its own prey. Its white belly looks like the light color of the sky to fish looking up. During a dive, a loon's back blends with the ripple effect of underwater light. So whether hunting or being hunted, a loon is well camouflaged.

# Feathered and Oiled

A loon spends most of its life on water colder than its body temperature. To stay warm, it has a thick layer of insulating fat inside its skin. Outside its skin, the loon wears a coat of soft, fluffy feathers called **down**. A dense layer of **contour feathers**, or outer feathers, covers the down like a raincoat to keep the loon dry.

To waterproof its feathers a loon **preens,** or grooms, its feathers with its bill, applying oil to its plumage several times a day. The oil is made in the loon's **uropygial** (yur-oh-PIE-jee-ahl) **gland**, on its lower back above its tail. Using its bill, the loon squeezes the gland and spreads the oil over its feathers like a sunbather putting on suntan lotion. After applying the oil, the loon pulls its outer feathers between its closed bill to zip the **barbs,** or tiny spikes, on the feathers shut like a zipper. When a loon's feathers are well oiled and zipped shut, they form a waterproof seal that keeps the loon dry.

BARB

SHAFT

CONTOUR
FEATHER

DOWN

UROPYGIAL GLAND

# oot Warmers

Loon feet dangle in cold water most of the time.

Numerous blood vessels circulate warm blood throughout both feet to keep them warm. In addition, the veins and arteries in a loon's legs lie next to each other. The blood going to its feet warms the blood going back to its body. At the same time, the blood returning to its body cools the blood going to its feet. This efficient heating and cooling system helps a loon keep warmth in its body.

A loon **thermoregulates**, or controls its body temperature, with its feet. A loon may **waggle**, or hold a foot out of the water, to help cool or warm itself.

# Bare Bones

Can you run fast? Can you jump high? Your **skeleton**, or bone structure, in part determines what you can do well. A loon is made for diving. Its pointed bill and heavy skull form an arrow shape. The loon's strong neck attaches to its head in a streamlined shape. The bird's wings fit snugly against its torpedo-shaped body and stay there while the loon is underwater. A loon's short thigh bones attach to its body under its wings and stick straight out. A loon has knees, but you can't see them. Its knees are inside the skin of its body. The knee holds the calf bone so it lies flat against the body. The loon's ankle and foot come out of the skin near its tail and are the only parts of a loon's leg that move freely. This position at the rear is great for swimming and diving but not so good for walking, much less for running or jumping!

## ACTIVITY

To see what it is like to walk like a loon, squat down. Hold your knees against you. Keep your ankles together and try to waddle forward. Whoa! That's hard to do! A loon also finds this hard to do, so it only goes on land to nest.

# ancy Footwork

Would diving flippers help you swim faster and dive deeper? A loon wears a natural pair of diving flippers. Each large foot has four toes with leathery webbing spread between the three long front toes. A loon's foot at rest is closed and drawn up close to its body. To swim, it pushes both feet back at the same time. A loon doesn't dog-paddle, or alternate its feet to swim. When the loon pushes its feet back, the soft webbing between its toes opens wide, enabling it to push as much water as possible. To reduce drag, the toes close when the foot comes forward. All this makes the loon a fast swimmer and a good diver.

**ACTIVITY**

To see what it is like to paddle like a loon, gently spread your fingers wide and press both hands down and back behind you. When you draw your hands forward to your sides, curl your fingers together. Now you are paddling like a loon.

# ow Rider

Large waves may capsize a boat, but large waves can't capsize a loon. A loon is a heavy bird, so it rides low in the water. Its bones are denser and heavier than other birds' bones are, and strong calf and chest muscles for swimming and flight add even more weight.

From its low-riding position, a loon can easily submerge. It does not need to jump up to plunge under like some diving birds do. To get ready for a dive, a loon squeezes air from its plumage by pressing its wings tightly against its sides. This also forces air out of its internal air sacs, balloonlike parts of the loon's breathing system that lie along its backbone. These are filled with air when the loon floats on the surface. Special nose and throat valves close to keep water out of its lungs. Then the loon puts its head down, kicks its feet, and slides smoothly under without a splash.

## ACTIVITY

To see how a loon's heavy weight gives it stability in water, fill a balloon with air and another balloon with water. Place the balloons in water. Make gentle waves. The balloon with air will toss and turn in the waves. The balloon with water will ride low in the water and be more stable.

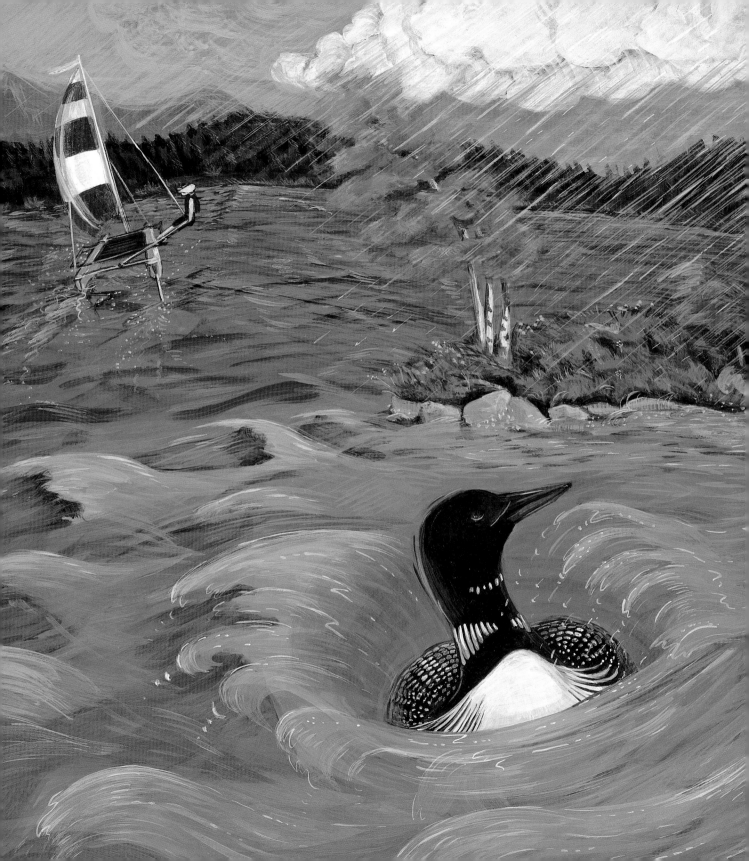

# eep-Sea Diver

A loon can stay underwater a long time. It stores lots of oxygen in its blood and muscles, and it can use its lungs like a scuba tank. Although a loon can stay underwater more than five minutes, the average dive is about one minute long. Most dives are less than 20 feet deep, which is usually deep enough for a loon to catch its prey.

Water is heavy—one gallon of water weighs eight pounds. How can a loon survive the weight of the water, or **water pressure,** during deep dives? A loon's rib cage can contract and expand. On the surface, when its air sacs are filled with air, the loon's ribs spread wide. During a dive its ribs squeeze together to form a strong structure that can withstand the weight of the water.

# one Fishing

A loon is **diurnal**, meaning it hunts during the day and rests at night. To find its food, a loon swims on the surface of the water with its bill and eyes underwater **peering,** or looking for prey. A loon's eyes are on the sides of its head, so each eye sees a different view. This is called **monocular vision**, which helps a loon spot prey from both sides. The loon's brain understands the two different views it sees, but because the views do not completely overlap in front, the loon has a hard time judging the exact position of its prey. Just before striking out, a loon moves its head back and forth to bring its food into focus. When a loon spots its prey, it dives. If a loon catches up with small prey, it sucks it in underwater like a vacuum cleaner. If it sees large prey, it swims after it and grabs it with its bill.

## ACTIVITY

To experience what it's like to see like a loon, hold one finger at arm's length in front of your face. Cover one eye and look, then open it and cover the other. Your finger seems to move against the background even though you know it's in the same place. Now focus both eyes on your finger. Notice how with both eyes you can better see where your finger is in relation to the background behind it.

# Dinner Is Served

A loon may look like it could spear its food, but it doesn't. It grasps fish crosswise in its bill. Both the top and bottom of a loon's bill can move, so a loon has a strong grip. The inside of its mouth is rough like sandpaper to help it hold on to slippery fish. When a loon catches a large fish, it brings it to the surface so it can turn the food to go down its throat headfirst. A loon swallows its food whole. Its throat stretches to allow a large fish to slide into its stomach, like a snake swallowing a mouse. A loon doesn't have many taste buds, and it doesn't care that it is eating live fish, guts and all.

A loon's stomach digests soft food easily. Its **gizzard**, the muscular part of the stomach, grinds bones and other hard bits of food into small pieces. To help grind, the loon swallows small pebbles. On the ocean, a loon swallows saltwater with every feeding. Large glands above its eyes remove the extra salt from its blood. All winter the thick, salty liquid drips out its nostrils like a continual runny nose.

# Nature's Perfect Submarine

When you play tag, how do you avoid being caught? A loon has a special way to escape called **sinking**. It lowers itself into the water by squeezing air out of its plumage and air sacs. A loon can sink until only its head is out of the water like a periscope. Then the loon can watch for danger without being seen. If the danger gets too close, the loon can sink deeper and disappear without a trace.

If a loon has to fight to defend itself, it uses its sharp, pointed bill as a weapon. A loon bill is made from **keratin**, the same substance as your fingernails. If a part of a loon's bill breaks off, it may slowly grow back.

# ast Flier

Flying is serious business for a loon. It cannot swoop and soar like an eagle, or make quick turns like a swallow. Its wings are too narrow. It only flies to get from one place to another using swift, steady wing beats. If a loon stopped flapping its wings, it would fall out of the sky.

A loon is heavy, but it can fly fast. It can match the speed of a car driving seventy-five miles per hour. A common loon can fly one and a half miles above the earth. Up that high, the cool, thin air lets the loon fly faster and keeps it from overheating.

A loon flies in a hunchback position, with its head and neck lower than its back, like the lowered nose of a jet. From below, a flying loon looks like a plus sign because its wings are attached to the center of its body. It can't pull its large feet in so they stick out behind its short tail. It puts its feet together like an airplane's rudder to help it steer.

# Ready for Takeoff

A loon flies well, but most loons have a hard time taking off. To lift its heavy weight a loon has to gain speed like a jet on a runway. The loon **patters**, or runs into the wind across the surface of the water, flapping its wings. Its water runway may need to be as much as a quarter mile long. A red-throated loon is lighter in weight for its wing size than other loons, so it can take off without a runway.

Once in the air, a loon climbs slowly. If a lake is surrounded by tall trees or hills a loon spirals upward like a jet circling an airport. To land, it spirals downward. A loon has to land on water because it lands belly first. If a loon tried to land on its feet it would fall over. A loon changes its **flight feathers**, the long stiff feathers on the ends of its wings, along with the rest of its feathers every year when it molts. A red-throated loon changes its flight feathers in the fall, but other loons molt in the spring. New flight feathers take up to six weeks to grow. During this time the loon cannot fly, but it can still swim and dive until its flight feathers grow back.

# The Dating Game

Loon pairs live apart during the winter, but in spring they usually return to the same lake where they raised their chicks the year before. Red-throated loons need only a small pond for nesting. Other species typically need a bigger lake. If one of the loons in a pair doesn't return, the remaining loon will likely pick a new mate. If challenged by another loon, the male will chase the challenger away by **rowing**, splashing across the water's surface while paddling with its wings. The stronger loon will claim the territory.

During loon **courtship,** when a loon chooses a mate, the pair swim, bob, dip, and dive together. After courtship, loons mate several times over a few days on the shoreline. During mating they trample the grass and reeds down, forming the foundation of their nest. They may continue to add nesting material after the eggs are laid.

# Baby-Sitting

The female loon lays two large, speckled eggs up to three days apart. In most species, both the male and female **incubate**, or sit on the eggs to keep them warm. Incubation takes up to four weeks. The loon gently pushes the eggs under its belly, turning the eggs to keep them evenly warm.

Several times a day, the loon takes a break or trades places with its mate. A loon gets on and off its nest carefully so it doesn't accidentally push the eggs off the nest with its large feet. Eggs can also be lost if high water floods the nest. Foxes, raccoons, otters, and birds such as gulls, crows, ravens, or jaegers sometimes steal loon eggs. A loon pair can lay another **clutch**, or batch of eggs, if it is still early in the summer. If danger threatens its nest, a loon hides by lowering its head. If the danger remains, the loon may **penguin dance**, charging across the water at the intruder with its chest raised and wings flat against its sides in an attempt to frighten the danger away.

# Delivery Day

A newly hatched chick is about the size of a lemon. Its body is covered with soft, fluffy down. It doesn't have flight feathers so its wings look like little arms. The **egg tooth**, a small, pointed bump on the top of its beak that it used to break out of its shell, disappears as the chick grows. After hatching, a chick stays on the nest just long enough to dry off. Then its parents coax it into the water by offering it a tiny fish. One parent removes the eggshell and **egg sac**, the thick inner lining of the egg, from the nest so that the smell doesn't attract predators before the second egg hatches the next day.

A chick can swim on its first day of life. It is safer in the water where the parents can better protect it. One parent cares for the chick while the other parent continues incubation. When both chicks are hatched, the loon family leaves the nest for good. Loon chicks may not feel land under their feet again for another year or more.

# Piggyback Rides

Have you ever had a piggyback ride? For the first weeks of life, a loon chick gets a piggyback ride whenever it is cold or tired. This keeps the chick warm while it sleeps and protects it from underwater predators like snapping turtles and big fish.

Loon parents feed the chick for up to two months. As the chick grows it learns how to dive and catch its own food. It takes a lot of fish to feed a loon family. A pair of loons with two chicks can eat two tons of fish in one summer. All this good food helps the chick grow. It soon outgrows its first set of down and grows a new, thicker coat. In mid- to late summer, the chick grows a set of gray feathers, complete with flight feathers. At about three months old, the chick learns to fly. Flapping its wings, the chick races across the water on stiff legs. The first short flights end in crash landings. After a few more days of practice, the chick can fly as well as its parents do.

# Birds of a Feather Flock Together

In late autumn, a chick is ready to migrate. By this time, the adult male may have left the nesting lake. Sometimes even the adult female has left. When the chick is ready, it too will leave the lake. Loons migrate during the day, flying in small, loose groups. At night they **raft up**, or gather with other loons, on a large lake or river to feed and rest. The journey to the ocean may take several days.

A **juvenile,** or young loon, stays on the coast to feed and grow for up to three years. Then the loon grows its breeding plumage and returns to its **natal area**, where it hatched. It finds a mate on a lake or hangs out with other nonbreeding loons on a nearby lake. It migrates back and forth from its ocean winter home to its lake summer home each year for the rest of its life and may live to be twenty to thirty years old.

# Living with Loons

A few years ago people noticed that there weren't as many loons as there used to be. Humans are responsible for much of this population decline. **Acid rain**, which is rain polluted by the exhaust of burning fossil fuels, can also harm loons by killing the fish that loons like to eat. Oil spills from ships can kill hundreds of loons at once. Some loons get caught in commercial fishing nets and drown. Dams can flood loon habitat. Homes or cabins built on lakeshores may disturb or destroy nest sites. Careless boating can chase a loon from its nest or territory. Loons can get tangled in fishing line or hurt by fishing hooks. If a loon swallows **lead sinkers**, weights put on the end of fishing line, the lead will poison the loon.

MONTROSE REGIONAL LIBRARY
320 SO. 2ND ST.
MONTROSE, CO 81401

#  Helping Loons

Today many people help loons. **Wildlife biologists**, people who study animals, may **band** a loon, capturing it and putting an identification ring on its leg before releasing it. The bird is then studied to learn where it goes and what it does. In areas where loons have lost their natural nesting places, people may set up artificial **nesting platforms** to help loons nest.

Many groups have formed to help loons. Some areas have **"Loon Rangers,"** people who watch a loon's nest and put signs around the nest that ask others to please stay back. If a loon's lake and ocean homes are clean and healthy, all a loon needs is an undisturbed place to nest and care for its chicks.

# LOON SPECIES

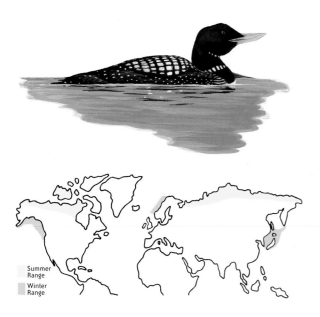

## YELLOW-BILLED LOON   *Gavia adamsii*

The yellow-billed loon earned its name from the color of its large, yellow, upturned bill. Its scientific name, *Gavia adamsii* (GAH-vee-ah AD-ums-ih-eye), means "seabird named in honor of Edward Adams," an Englishman who explored the Arctic in the 1800s.

A yellow-billed loon is the largest loon. It weighs up to sixteen pounds. It is more than three feet long, with a wingspan up to six feet. Its large bill and the feathered crown of its head make it look bold. Its white necklace and black-and-white checkered back add to its bold look.

Yellow-billed loons spend their summers in the Arctic regions of North America and Asia. In North America, they winter on the Pacific coast of the United States and Canada. In Europe, they spend their winters on the Atlantic coastline. In Asia, they winter near Japan and China.

## COMMON LOON   *Gavia immer*

A common loon is called "common" because it lives farther south than other loons, so more people see it. Its scientific name, *Gavia immer* (GAH-vee-ah IM-mer), means "seabird that immerses," or goes underwater.

A common loon is the second largest loon. It weighs eight to twelve pounds and is three feet long, with a wingspan of up to five feet. The common loon has a black, straight bill and a steep forehead. Its black head shines with a green iridescence.

Common loons spend their summers in Greenland, Iceland, and across the northern part of North America. This is the only loon species to nest in the United States outside of Alaska. Most common loons winter along the Pacific Coast from Alaska to Mexico and along the Atlantic Coast from Canada to the Gulf of Mexico. Some winter in the Great Lakes. Common loons from Greenland and Iceland winter near northern Europe.

Summer Range
Winter Range

## ARCTIC LOON  *Gavia arctica*

The Arctic loon gets its common and scientific names from living in the Arctic. *Gavia arctica* (GAH-vee-uh ARC-tih-kuh) means "seabird from the Arctic." In Europe and Asia this loon is called the black-throated diver.

An Arctic loon weighs four to six pounds. The size of a large duck, it is about two and a half feet long with a four-foot wingspan. Its straight, black bill and narrow, sloping forehead give it an elegant look. Its gray head and black throat have an iridescent green sheen.

Arctic loons spend their summers in Alaska, northern Europe, and Russia. They winter on the coasts of Europe and Asia. A few migrate to the northern Mediterranean Sea and the Black and Caspian Seas.

## PACIFIC LOON  *Gavia pacifica*

The Pacific loon's common and scientific names come from its winter home, the Pacific Ocean. *Gavia pacifica* (GAH-vee-uh pah-CIH-fih-kuh) means "seabird from the Pacific."

If you think Arctic and Pacific loons look alike, you're not alone. Until 1985 scientists thought they were the same species. Today Arctic and Pacific loons are classified separately because they do not **interbreed**, or mate and have chicks together.

A Pacific loon is also a little smaller than an Arctic loon. A Pacific loon weighs three to five pounds and is about two and a half feet long with a four-foot wingspan. A purple iridescence shimmers on its silver gray head and black throat.

Pacific loons summer in Alaska and western Canada. They winter along the Pacific coast of North America as far south as Mexico.

Summer Range

Winter Range

## RED-THROATED LOON   *Gavia stellata*

The red-throated loon gets its common name from the red patch on the front of its throat. Its scientific name, *Gavia stellata* (GAH-vee-uh STEH-lah-tuh), means "seabird that is starry." The scientist who gave this loon its scientific name thought the red patch looked like a star. Some observers think the red-throated loon's back looks like a starry sky. In Scotland, a red-throated loon is called a rain-goose because it calls before a storm.

The red-throated loon is the smallest of the loons, weighing only three to four pounds. It is about two feet long with a wingspan of about three feet. The red-throated loon has a narrow, sloping forehead, with a slender, black, up-turned bill. Unlike the other loon species, it doesn't have a checkered back in summer and its neck stripes are on the back of its head.

Red-throated loons nest farther north than any other loon. Their nesting grounds circle the globe and include the northernmost parts of North America, Greenland, Iceland, Europe, Russia, and China. In winter, red-throated loons live along the coasts of North America, Europe, and Asia. A few winter in the Great Lakes region in the northern United States and southern Canada and on the Black and Caspian Seas in Europe and Russia.

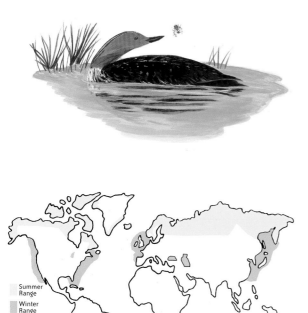

Summer Range

Winter Range

# LOON RESOURCE LIST

## LOON WEB SITES

These are some of the organizations that help care for loons. Some of the Web sites are sponsored by the government, some by an association, and a few by volunteers.

### Alaska Fish and Wildlife Service
www.r7.fws.gov/mbm/loons
*All five loon species live in Alaska. At this site see a photo of a red-throated loon, and find out how Alaska cares for all of its loons.*

### Anchorage Audubon
www.alaska.com/akcom/loons
*Check out the Connors Lake LoonCam during nesting season for live images of a breeding pair of Pacific loons hatching their eggs. Click on the "Still Image Archive" at other times of the year.*

### British Columbia Tourist Services
www.britishcolumbia.com/wildlife/wildlife/birds/cw/cw_commonloon.html
*Learn how to identify loons in the field with this easy-to-use loon profile guide.*

### California Loon Watch
www.hometown.aol.com/djl4loons
*Could you ever see a loon near a palm tree? Visit this site and click on "Loon Multimedia Page." Then scroll down to see how a loon spends its winter. You'll also find the true story of a Pacific loon that was rescued from an oil spill.*

### Canadian Lakes Loon Survey
www.bsc-eoc.org/cllsmain.html
*If you're a loon, Canada is the place to be. Find out how some people there protect their loons from raccoons.*

### Journey North
www.learner.org/north/spring2002/species/loon/
*Could you have a loon for a pet? Why do some loons fly with their mouths open? On this site you'll find the answers to these questions and more, as well as maps of loon migration taken from actual student sightings. Teachers will love the "Teacher Tip" section. Go to "Lessons, Activities and Information" for recordings of loon yodels.*

## Maine's Biodiversity Institute

www.briloon.org

*Watch a pair of loons incubate and hatch chicks on this site's WebCam. Find lots of loon facts on this site, as well as printable common loon range and migration maps.*

## Michigan Loon Preservation Association

www.michiganloons.org/

*See a flying loon when you open this site, then click on "Biology," and find the big word "originated" in the text. Click on it to find a time line of bird evolution.*

## Minnesota Department of Natural Resources

www.dnr.state.mn.us

*To see an X ray of a loon with a lead sinker in its stomach go to this site and type "Get the Lead Out" in the* Search DNR *box near the top of the page. You'll see that it doesn't take much lead to poison a loon.*

## Montana Loon Society

www.montanaloons.org

*See photos of children helping loons, and learn more about "Loon Rangers" on this site.*

## New Hampshire Loon Preservation Committee

www.loon.org

*Read "A Day in the Life of a Loon" on this site and find a great photo of a common loon in winter plumage.*

## New York Audubon

www.audubonintl.org/programs/asny/loon.htm

*Find out just how big loon feet really are and other fun trivia facts on this site.*

## New York State's Adirondack Cooperative Loon Program

www.adkscience.org/loons

*What's all the fuss about the call of the loon? Go to the bottom of the home page and click on "Loons." Then click on "Loon Natural History." Page two of "Loon Natural History" has a superb feature where you can listen to loon calls: a hoot, wail, tremolo, and yodel.*

## Vermont Loon Recovery Project

www.anr.state.vt.us/reflect/july16.htm

*Have you ever been in loon territory and wondered what you could do to help loons? On this site learn some important things everyone can do when visiting loon country.*

*Washington's Loon Lake Loon Association*
www.loons.org
*You'll find lots of common loon photos in this site's "Photo Gallery." To see a banded loon, click on "Loon Activities."*

*Northern Wisconsin Tourism, Travel, and Outdoors*
www.northernwisconsin.com/loons.htm
*Find lots of answers to common loon questions on this site.*

## LOON BOOKS

*The Common Loon: Spirit of the Northern Lakes.* Judith W. McIntyre. Minneapolis: University of Minnesota Press, 1988.
*Written by one of the world's leading loon biologists, this book takes a scientific and in-depth look at the common loon. Includes research and graphs.*

*Loons.* Aubrey Lang and Wayne Lynch. Toronto: Firefly Books, 1996.
*Large photos and short, to-the-point text by this husband-and-wife writer/wildlife photographer team make this book a fun way to learn about loons. Includes photos of all species.*

*Loons.* Roy Dennis. Stillwater, Minn.: Voyageur Press, 1993.
*Written by a biologist from Scotland, this book takes a factual look at loons, spending equal time on each loon species.*

*Love of Loons.* Kate Crowley and Mike Link. Stillwater, Minn.: Voyageur Press, 1988.
*Find lots of common loon folklore and legends in this easy-to-read but scientific book.*

*Shared Spirits: Wildlife and Native Americans.* Dennis Olson. Minnetonka, Minn.: NorthWord Press, 1999.
*Find a loon legend, as well as other animal legends, in this fun book.*

*The Uncommon Loon.* Terry McEneaney. Flagstaff: Northland Publishing, 1991.
*Take an "uncommon" look at the common loon with this factual, thorough book.*

## LOON BOOKS FOR CHILDREN

*Loon Magic for Kids.* Tom Klein. Minnetonka, Minn.: NorthWord Press, 1991.

*Loons.* Patrick Merrick. Channhassen, Minn.: The Child's World, Inc., 2000.

# INDEX

—MICHAEL GALLACHER PHOTO

—RICHARD T. TURLEY PHOTO

## ABOUT THE AUTHOR

**Donna Love** lives in Seeley Lake, Montana, where her husband, Tim, is the District Ranger for the Seeley Lake Ranger District on the Lolo National Forest. For the past seven years she has watched a loon family hatch and raise chicks on the lake outside her door. To help with loon conservation she serves as an officer for the Montana Loon Society and speaks statewide on behalf of Montana's loons. Using her art education background she developed a children's loon program, "Loon Tunes and Water Balloons," for use in grade schools. This program formed the basis of her book.

## ABOUT THE ILLUSTRATOR

**Joyce Mihran Turley** has illustrated books on many topics for readers of all ages. Joyce discovered her artistic talents in high school, but chose a career in engineering because she loved mathematics as well. She retired from engineering and soon returned to her artwork, establishing her own illustration studio, Dixon Cove Design. Raised in upstate New York, Joyce has lived in the Colorado foothills of the Rocky Mountains for over twenty years. She regularly observes deer, lizards, eagles, and coyotes outside the picture windows of her home studio. No loons have been sighted so far!

# Mountain Press Books for Young Readers

_____A Field Guide to Nearby Nature: Fields and Woods
      of the Midwest and East Coast
                $15.00
                *Ages 8 and up*

_____LOONS: Diving Birds of the North      $12.00
                *Ages 8 and up*

_____Nature's Yucky! Gross Stuff That Helps Nature Work   $10.00
                *Ages 5 and up*

_____OWLS: Whoo are they?      $12.00
                *Ages 8 and up*

_____Sacagawea's Son: The Life of Jean Baptiste Charbonneau   $10.00
                *Ages 10 and up*

_____Spotted Bear: A Rocky Mountain Folktale      $15.00
                *Ages 5 and up*

_____Stories of Young Pioneers: In Their Own Words    $14.00
                *Ages 10 and up*

_____Tales of Two Canines: The Adventures of a Wolf and a Dog   $10.00
                *Ages 10 and up*

*Please include $3.00 shipping and handling for 1–4 books and $5.00 for 5 or more books.*

Send the books marked above. I have enclosed $_____

Name_____Phone_____

Address_____

City/State/Zip_____

☐ Payment enclosed (check or money order in U.S. funds)

Bill my:  ☐ VISA  ☐ MasterCard  ☐ American Express  ☐ Discover

Card No._____Exp. Date_____

Signature_____

## MOUNTAIN PRESS PUBLISHING COMPANY

Post Office Box 2399 / Missoula, Montana 59806

PHONE 406·728·1900 / FAX 406·728·1635 / TOLL FREE 1·800·234·5308

E-MAIL info@mtnpress.com / WEBSITE www.mountain-press.com